Blood Rivers
Poems of Texture From the Border

Poems by
Lisha Adela García

Blue Light Press ◆ 1st World Publishing

1st WORLD
PUBLISHING

San Francisco ◆ Fairfield ◆ Delhi

BLOOD RIVERS
POEMS OF TEXTURE FROM THE BORDER

Copyright ©2009 by Lisha Adela García

1ST WORLD LIBRARY
106 South Court Street
Fairfield, Iowa 52556
www.1stworldpublishing.com

BLUE LIGHT PRESS
1563 45th Avenue
San Francisco, California, 94122

BOOK AND COVER DESIGN
Melanie Gendron
www.melaniegendron.com

COVER ART
"Only an Egg America Reflected"
©2000 Melanie Gendron

COVER PHOTO
Babe Sarver
www.babesphotos.com

FIRST EDITION

LCCN: 2009936291

ISBN: 978-1-4218-9134-7

This book is dedicated with love and *compasión*
to Adelaida Artola Allen (Yaya) and Adela Artola Allen,
grandmother and mother, and all of our ancestors
on both sides of the border.

Acknowledgments

I would like to thank the many sources of creativity for my work including my family, Diane Frank of Bluelight Press, Vermont College's MFA program and the ghosts that haunt my labyrinth. I owe a great debt to *mi madre*, Dr. Adela Artola Allen, and my children, Carlos Mariano García and Daniela Cristina García for being constant lights and word fodder. *Gracias Mil y que Dios los bendiga siempre.* Special kudos go to my sister, Shannon Applegate and brother-in-law, Daniel Robertson, for all their encouragement. I would like to thank my many friends and writing buddies too numerous to mention individually, but of special import would be Rozanna Mendoza, Dr. Rafaela SantaCruz, Emilio Hinojosa, Deena Metzger, Mary Fillmore, Louisa Howe, Marco Antonio Jeréz and Lana Hechtman Ayers. Special thanks to my writing groups: Ten Bluelight Press classmates; the Tejanas: Carmen Tafolla, Velma Nanka Bruce, Aida Pineda Pierson, and Martha McCabe; The Piper Poets: Dorothy Direnzi, Roberta Burnett, Kristina Morgan, Patricia Bates, Brooks Michalik, Cathy Capozzoli and Francie Noyes.

Gracias Mil also goes to my *Tía* Susy, Susana Romero Artola de González for accompanying me on the journey with unconditional love and support since I was the flower girl at her wedding.

TABLE OF CONTENTS

I

BORDERED IN SKULLS

A Woman's Hands in a Time of War

"Let the rubble be our evidence. . ."
—Heather McHugh

When I place my hands together,
meeting palm against palm, and press
so hard my knuckles turn white,
I know I have squeezed the screams

out of my prayers. Together, all the women
I know, force their hands onto
their abdomens, a mother's signal
to God that our wombs

crave new seedlings, bread.
War is too long,
dreaming, the only reality.
A man from America took a picture

of me once, placing both my hands
on the space between my birth
button and my husband's peace,
pressing so hard that hope escaped along

with the hunger. My hands change
positions often, clutching stones to throw
at the stray men who prey on our children
or to scare the vultures near by. These hands

molded clay into water jars before,
and now they carry bodies with faces
I do not know, wrapped in scraps for the heaps
to be sorted later. I hope other women will

do this for my love, for my village.
My fingers curve to write the words that hold
my skin onto a sheet of paper, a letter that gets folded
over and over as if holding my love has limits

within the creases. When I get angry at God,
my hands tighten into fists and I hit my thighs
and do not breathe.
I fear the life I hold in might escape

with the tears. I strap my breasts down
with cloths left over from birthing
dead babies. I visit the old graves of the city
and make room for the new.

My grandmother lived through war, and she said
sometimes it takes years before the layers in the rubble
reveal the underbelly of why
it was worth living at all.

St. Francis in Mesilla

I speak from the pecan groves of Mesilla
and do not relive the feel of stomped boots
on my flesh. The wind sings the memories

of the dead beneath my feet everywhere I walk.
War tames the sassy wildness of the rich
who justify themselves later by becoming Buddhists

who sell meditation tapes. They come here and set up
retreat centers that charge a lot of money for peace.
Penitents come and go and find no more

answers than a cracked pecan shell on the ground,
a brown casket opened to expose a delicate white center
that waits for release. Just food for the crows.

They pay to believe silence and bells
will maintain their sanity. It is enough for me
to search my El Greco book and look at his painting

of St. Francis talking to his skull about the fragility
and impermanence of it all. I can hear him say, "Brother Sun
and Sister Moon, I don't need to go to war to learn this."

And me, I just do laundry. The blood of the committed
is washed from their socks as they hang blind
on the line and face the lightning all alone.

My Mother Wants Me to Explain

For Dr. Adela Artola Allen

My mother wants me to write poems
about the different borders between
Anglo and Mexican culture.
No amamos igual, no sentimos igual.

Tell how most Americans
don't laugh at death or write *Calaveras*
about the President, or make *tamales* at Christmas.

Explain when non-Mexicans buy
every ingredient fresh to cook our food,
the chile against their skin,
their tongues can never taste the conquest—
write about that.

My poems are about what unite us, I reply,
heart to eyes, throat to guttural survival.

But we still speak the language of Cervantes
she counters, Cervantes and Nahuatl, Zapotec
Purepecha and Mayan. They speak
in Northern, Southern or Mid-western.

Explain the importance of the hands
of women who choose to tell their stories
in the colors of their *huipiles*
and wouldn't dream of looking the same
store after store, mall after mall.

Speak with your fingers to tell the story
of coyotes and owls,
why birds always arrive in the Americas,
and carry spirits on their wings.

Tell why hatred
for differences has also claimed us,
why it is important
that bougainvilleas have thorns —

Speak for all of us still here,
and for those who have been here
so long they have lost their Spanish,
who hear the *Mariachis*, the cantos,
and have forgotten the nuances of our songs.

MEXICO CITY

For Mercedes Arratia de Medina

The serpents inside the glass slither
on the information about information
eating itself. Quetzalcoatl, plumed serpent god,
is here and whips his smog feathers against
the window panes. All anyone sees and hears
is transportation transcendence.

Art will be about the fucking of information.
It will look like skeletal fumes choking
the best of the Polanco Princesses, blue
in their penthouses. It will rebel against
nuance. Everything will be a clear
revenge of the European invasion.

Skyless search engines will hunt for souls.
I am the stone grasshopper kept alive,
but frozen in time in Chapultepec Park,
my long black tongue, a computer
chewing the lessons of history against traffic, asking,
México, what remains of your belly of mercy?

ALFONSINA WALKS INTO THE SEA

"Silence is the perfect water." —*Phillip Levine*
For poet, Alfonsina Storni

I am now one cut breast,
an upright timber
without the appendage that suckled
poison to my heart and gave
my poems to the world.

I want this wood, this body
to flow to the sea, flesh bark
to be eaten by sharks, not so different
from what men already
ravaged, my bones
fodder for a coral reef.

A slow walk, at first
I stumble,
caught against a rock
pushed back,
the shore still reachable.
Then I see my son's contorted face
at my slow death.

This is not an uncharted choice
between the hand of the shore
and the water. I choose what
is left behind in Buenos Aires,
the gypsy comes with me.
It seems the sand moves forward,
or does the sea retreat?

My nurse cries out from the land!
Warming, my writing fingers
grab a branch, my feet lift
out with the tide. I won't look
back like Lot's wife.

Memories leave in gentle
moonlit laps, a poet's
watermark, the last view.

I ask the stars to pray,
water breathes at last
silence, a funnel to swallow.

This Stone Will Speak

As the high Maya priestess of Chi Chen Itzá,
I rule the temple, and I am dying.
Before I leave, I have carved a stella
of all my mistakes, to be placed
on the east wall of the Nunnery.
It is hell revealed, my life.

This is the only way to escape the priests,
my tribe and the indifference of heaven
that has tethered minds
to the tradition of human sacrifice.

My story is bordered in the skulls
of the warriors that gave their
lives for the poets.
When my bones have burned
and I enter the chrysalis of heaven,
my errors will be placed in plain view.

What I have hidden
will be revealed
in stone that faces the sunrise.

What I have endured,
will be remembered
in stone that shadows with sunset.

All will know why at the end,
I stood alone with the *quetzal*
to be burned.

A Wake

To be awake and view a dead person.
The trail a boat leaves in the water,
a small wave. Jet stream of an airplane,
cloud exhaust across the blue. Imitations
of God making souls out of nothing.

Neon red noises were the last metaphor
heard by my friend, a poet in Earth School.
The final moments, a sour pentameter
that reached the brain before it went dead.

A wake, a nice ceremony
for those that survive the plucking of prey.
I am here, fully present
to the life of a poet by the water—
all the snow melted,
spiders weaving snowflakes
and freezing them for spring.

San Fernando Cathedral, San Antonio de Bejar, Día de los Muertos

In the theater of the Mass, the obligatory *Señoras*
of Guadalupe stand in the front pews
fingers on rosary beads, clicking. They are caustic
to outsiders who come to see the marble
encasings of Bowie and that lawless Kentuckian
fortunate enough to die at the Alamo. In front
of these tombs, brown hands reach to pin a *milagro*,
a miracle of thanks, on the robe of the Black Christ.
Ana's thanks for her escape from the death squads
of Guatemala. San Antonio is a safe place
where the Hispanic brush says we all look alike.

Once a year the Rabbi comes and cries to God
without his minyans. A Protestant female priest joins him
and forgets the Pope does not like women in charge
of God. They stand next to our little Father David
and pray for the dead. *Día de los Muertos*, All Souls Day.
We gather to remember the politics of the moment, the barbed
wire of borders and the names of all those bodies who
have no families here to grieve. A daughter of El Salvador
carries a child in a rebozo and places a white rose
at the altar of the *Virgen de Guadalupe*,
Patroness of the Américas, tied with a red
ribbon, the name of her dead father
scrawled on its shiny side.

The *Señoras* of Guadalupe adjust the lace
they still wear on their heads
and, with the rest of us, are asked to remember
what it's like to be unwanted. The lawyer passes the basket
and the retired colonel helps with communion.
We all sing together, Jews, Christians, tourists,
frightened immigrants and me knowing death
has its eye on our sockets and will hook us
home, heart or no heart, hero or no hero,
gold marigolds, *cempasuchil*, to guide our way.

CORSET

We all have our corset of wounds:
not reaching water in the desert,
being suddenly blind, or just dying
from the inside out,
as fleshy parts bask
in cashmere and grey silk.

Age trades one type of locura for another:
la droga, tequila, pastillas, prayer,
numbing what inner or outer slaughters
we cannot control.

We have cast ourselves through
the gene pool onto the earth,
not knowing if we are
a child of sonata
or the mold of a holocaust.

II

VIA SACRA

WOMEN ARE DOORS

"Woman is the door that reconciles us with the world."
—*Octavio Paz*

Women are doors
framed *huipiles*
embroidered tunics
of stories and colors
for prayers to heaven
or splintered lintels
aged by limited
endurance

Essential barometers
against storms
against shame
offices   orifices   privacy
with knockers locks and keys
bathrooms   sex
bleeding not just for the moon.

Gateways to shelter
hiding scribbled notes in door jambs
at the end of a concrete path
at the beginning of a porch rocker
keeping the family stories
red maple leaves on virgin snow,

gathering grace.

FROM HEAVEN TO LIFE

I didn't want to come back to a body.
My ancestors called me forth
from the sand. They molded fire-lit clay
and attached it to my rib cage,
sang to the fate threads,
long as the rim of the Grand Canyon,
a mural for my story.

I heard them call my totems—
horse, hummingbird, bear and falcon.
They whispered cantos to settle
in my bones and erase the memories
of previous times my fingers dipped
into the Havasupi river of life.

Again, to be one of millions
of humans pecking at the ground,
convinced that casting lots for a body
was similar to jumping off a mesa
and told not to focus
on sharp green granite below.

Amidst the protest,
the dervish dance begins
with first breath scream.
Fingers now long for rose petals
near an herb garden. Eyes
water anew with fear at the smell
of fire on the Mogollon plateau,
new desperate cries as a daughter.

It won't stop until the death trill,
and the stones thrust upon my grave can't hold me.   17

My Moon

If the Father is the sun,
and Mother is earth,
then moon is the holy ghost
that guides my plight.

She bends the light in sharp angles
around buildings and cityscapes,
luminarias on cement for homeless people,
yellow haze to see labels on the cans
they consume, and shadow witness death.

Every rotation, invisible threads
connect to the cycle of waves
and I come into my moon.
I transform into magnet woman,
create a tempest wind
to quench the overwrought,
and men become afraid.

Illuminated round by the sun,
I become predator,
hunt with owls and hawks
on the unsuspecting.
I touch madness and survey lists
of suicides and murders.
I wait all year for October to pull blood
from bodies that soak the ground
and call myself,
                    Harvest.

I speak directly to stars
about alchemical lust-dust.
I shine on hemlock and nightshade,
only once, every twenty-eight days,
I am full.

VIA SACRA

How do we know the stars
within us are not dark
wings from a dead moon,
ravens on white
catching ghosts that give a damn?

Stardust specks that hide
inside our casings,
blood rivers we carry
where wind cannot touch
the goodness and darkness
measured by our angels,

zig zags of thunder
never spoken out loud.

Dreaming History

"History is the depository of great actions."
—Miguel de Cervantes

My history is scarred on my liver,
in my dreams and on the heart.
A sign with the word "hope"
hangs precariously from my pineal gland.
I have been told all writers share this shingle.

My history is stored in the eaves
of the houses where I have slept,
where dreams escape,
ask questions of the night ghosts
touch my cheek, whisper cantos.

This is why I know
when we dream of houses,
we are the houses.

Every night, I search for a story
in the library, dungeon, or garden,
following a music that drifts ahead of me
in a cloud. I search for safe ectoplasm
to bring back to the white pages
next to my blue bed.

I want my house near the water
to look up through the cottonwoods
and study the puzzles of the sky.

DIVINER

The rosetta of the pine cone
invites me in just to let me know
I am not part of its core.

Where is the diviner in the all or nothing
of the pine needle nest, that sacred
sustenance needed to harbor a seed?
I search for gold spirits
before my skin becomes
the toughest bark,
my steps the driest sod.

The wellspring of fate
is not spun in the night voices
of my grandmother, Yaya,
and my *tías*, whose hands
on my shoulders lull me
to the respite of their arms.

A compass of lavender
sage and a new breeze
in my ear says, rest daughter,
rest, and let us bring
on a blue jay's flight
the well augury to you.

ANCESTOR HANDS

The shape of my hand,
benedictions and curses
in the grooves of the grasp,
a challenge to any palm reader.

In the way crater water reflects clouds
for only a moment, I shake
my hand, my grandmother's hand,
and reach back to ancestor filaments
to find the perfect stone.

My wrist, with an expert fisherman's flick
sends the stone across the top of life,
a small death at every bounce
rippled   gentle   wake
a new image of my face,
a hand in the lake,
the eye of my heart.

QUIZÁS

Love is a waltz
starving death for a moment.
A tango,
a bouquet of rose thorns,
the landscape of you
awakening
to courage:
the glass in the mirror
is not me
the glass in the window
is not life.
Thousands of windows
opening
closing
to the rain.
It is all a guess
when the sahuaro blooms.

Biblical Musings

"Non Omnis Moriar. I shall not wholly die."
—Dante Algieri

"You will do these things and more–
it has been given unto you" – me I think,
though I've taken more to the mysteries
of sorrow and squandered the psalms.

"In the house of the Lord there are
many mansions." I am searching
for the room where baptism
sorcery brings peace.

Was the water in the font
more mystical after they washed Jesus' feet?
I do not ask God for anything.
I ask God for everything.

Serenity on the angel's wing eludes me.
I want to remember the beauty of white roses
that give grace and rekindle my ability to weep.

25

Recurring Dream of My Geography

The closest depiction,
Frida Kahlo's painting of the two
Fridas: mirror images, they sit
in opposite chairs, hearts exposed
with a thin tube, a blood line
connecting one heart to another
across the room.

I also wear white.
The right half sits on a teal and pink
wooden chair with white doves, painted peace.
The left sits on a blue and red chair,
with silver stars and dollar signs.
The blood tube that unites my hearts
has a measured leak in the middle,
droplets falling to river
my own Rio Grande, Río Bravo.

My whole life is the geography between the chairs:
two countries, two cultures, two languages.
My ghosts have no trouble reconciling my two selves;
they see coherence from their perch
outside space and time. I have only
one heart really, beating for both,
fence bruised.

WATER GOURDS

As told to me by Hopi elder, Vernon Masayessva, Black Mesa Trust

The fourth world is coming to an end—
we have broken the cosmic balance
and have been judged dry
by the divine. The Hopi, as first
people, must kiva
and travel between worlds,
Sipapu, to reshape the balance.

We are all water gourds;
our river connects our body
together, ears to toes
just like oceans connect the land
and link us to the cosmic sea.
Water Serpent, the first being
is restless; the oceans are restless.

We are clouds,
water arrows of lightning
consecrating the world
in the six directions.
We must release the first energy,
bring back heaven on earth.

We have the same tools as the Hopi
of the first world. We have the seeds
of the first corn; we have a planting stick
now called technology;
we are the water in our gourds.

27

Hopi wait for the fifth world
when people of all colors
come to the center of the earth,
the southern side of the San Francisco
Peaks, to remake our pledge to the Katsinas,
to make peace for the water.

kiva— Hopi place for community decision making
Sipapu— the portal between one world and the next for the people.
Katsinas— benevolent spirit beings that accompany the Hopi

Afternoon at the Ranch in Oregon
With Anglo Relatives

for Shannon Applegate

No one thought to bring my umbilical
cord here and bury it in the earth
in the ways of my mother's people.
A forcible tie of my spirit
to this ground, where my half-sister
and her friends are now singing.
The porch of the oldest house in Oregon
sways with the moments
I have to borrow a culture, as mine fails me.
My circle might find these women trite
in their cowboy songs, but my father,
who is lost in the conversation
the dead have with themselves,
would be soothed by these harmonies.
I am sure he is listening.

Melinda's herb garden has lasted 100 years.
The water from the same well
escapes the lavender and leaves a visible
scar on my shoe to brand my blood.
The guitar provides the right tempo
to a loud hunter's crack in the empty
space before me. The ghosts
that know me, though I know them not,
follow me like the gunman shooting the dove
as it throws wide its wing exposing soft down.
Their silhouettes move rockers back and forth,
not visible, unpretentious at home with the breathing,
like me, trying music as a lei line to this earth.

The spiders in the pasture
have caught me for a moment in their webs;
they also think me a fly that belongs.
The wind is long with memory,
a soft feather held by a lover
removes hair from my face.
I feel lost to the bones of this place.
I wonder how many animals
would have to be sacrificed
before I could predict the future from their entrails.
I wonder what it would feel like
to not be lost in constant translation.

Socks

The top anthropologists have studied
my socks and found them warm
and caressing on the surface. I have hung them
on the clothesline, folded in half
and pinched shut with the revolver
of a clothespin. A *gancho* that swings
open and closed in what flows in the breeze
does not get generalized away.
Socks become hungry for the skeleton
dreams littering the ground that tempted fate
like the candy skulls of *Día de los Muertos*.
In the moonlight, the socks look
to each other for enlightenment,
want to form a circle rather than line up
where they can only see parts of each
other at the wind's whim.
I ask the right sock to lift its guitar
and sing me to my grave.
No shovel in the ground, I want
ash on the bluebird's wing.

LOT'S WIFE

"Who mourns one woman in a holocaust."
—Anna Akmatova

My name is the earth
that still bears witness,
the part God made leach into the ground
so nothing could ever grow again.
A reminder of disobedience
bound to the soil
practical for men's version of history.

An archeologist came close
to finding me once, but all he saw
were lilies blooming a few feet away,
my Easter in search
of the God of Women.

Had I lived,
I would have kept my daughters
from bearing children with their father,
and stopped the formation
of two warring tribes in this holy land.

Sacrifice is a woman's way,
a mother's. I am the example
for those who live in the past
and can't focus on the road ahead
one step in front of another, one day at a time.

Where was Lot's mercy;
where was his grief?
How convenient to say I had no faith—
to toss aside the wounds of mourning
my sons, my grandchildren—
no returning from the fire.

I had to smell the death smoke,
be sure they were gone
before I became a pillar
in remembrance to horror.
I am salt, the organic compound of life.

THE WAY OF LOVE

The Río Grande, a river
hugging both sides of my story,
my heritage floating back and forth
in the current, its tiny waves changing
direction when a body crosses
from one edge to another,
taking back its fluidity
in the renewed baptism
of two nation's politics.

The way the Sonoran desert halts
the flow of the river, and stores
water in barrel cactus and sahuaros,
a known refuge for the thirsty
who become entangled in thorns.

That I can name the air, the wind
of *El Niño*, that repaints the dunes
every night so you never step
twice in the same sand, a seabed
with no memory of your passing.

The smell of white copal
while I stand on a Spanish balcony
of an hacienda overlooking
the Mayan jungle.

Drums made with goat skins,
russet maracas filled with pumpkin
seeds that dance for the spirits
as I watch the sparks singe the night
from a bonfire in an arroyo.

A good story, with a beginning
and end, loved people sitting
around my dinner table,
watching the poetry of a Monarch Butterfly
journey south to Michoacan.

III

COYOTE LAUGHING

ADRIFT

Futility in the bones of my fingers
holding a pen. Is this where the cold
inability to write begins to crush paper?
As if I were the monarch butterfly
that descends, lives brightly
and then hides its patina
in the ivy frost of a garden.

Rainwater staccato is clear,
patient as the dusk,
inevitable as the peeling
of ashbark in winter.
There is a ruse of frivolity
in letting go of old skin
kneeling to the clouds,
a new color in each light.

I gather words, their sounds and stare down.
Possibilities in the round water of my glass
pass unheeded in swirls,
as if time had no portent—
as if my bones would not
fill the earth with roots.

SNAIL

My *brujas* are here,
those ladies that pray over me
and massage my ankles and feet
to let the tired spirits out.
This is when I realize
I carry my home with me
like a snail,
a snail that likes the graveyard
too much. I am standing on a headstone
looking at myself.
My clothes cling to my body
in pockets turned outward
and inward, in pain or joy,
depending on how much life
I can contain at the moment.
I see a man haunting graves,
razor scars all over his body,
his neck, the rope burn of oblivion.
Perhaps, this is why I like cemeteries,
especially in Paris.
They have all those white
temples I can't take with me.
So many snail shells left on the ground.

RED WHITE AND BLUE FEAR

The nerve endings of my culture
have been cemented over
with theft and treaties.
The history of conquest is clear,
once corn calls to our teeth
the neat rows of growth crack concrete.
Spanish is home again,
México Norte.

A bridge, a gate, a fence
so far not effective in keeping starving
ants from advancing.
A scar is now burnt into the soil
of the desert, vaporized human traffic.

Alma García, who is now a special consultant
for the Wall Street Journal
reports the following stories:
1) That her native language is now a felony.
2) In a capricious tribute to global investment,
   crosses pierce the Arizona desert.
3) That Bermuda grass, washed dishes
   and mangoes nicely sliced,
   packaged in plastic for shopping
   convenience are not responsible.

Alma is not responsible.
4) Aztlán, poured over, is still Aztlán.

She asks you, the viewers, if you hear
Coyote laughing at night?

40

BODEGA RICHES

In downtown Laredo, warehouses full of used clothes
are *trapos* piled high in mounds.
I scavenge for the right white blouse.

Hope is recycled from the land of supreme waste
to the streets of Monterrey, México where I sell
the newly pressed clothes on the street.

The mist off the Río Grande mixes with dust
for a second hand too-late feeling. I search
for a yellow pair of pants for Rosa, my client.

My fellow pickers and I speak Spanglish,
the Esperanto of choice for the natives
who can trace their roots back

to Lipan Apaches, Spanish Land Grants
and Jews fleeing the inquisition. Starting over, picking
rags at the *bodegas,* is to wait for a future

where your organs run on survival
fluid. I will use my *Pesos* to buy
rich peach roses only I will see.

FORCED OUT OF WORK, WAY PAST 40

The Ivy League pretty boys in D.C. cannot imagine tax dollars used for Maria Celia's brown hands to weave a cloth on a loom that got her a job with the tourists. Conquest budgets leave little for those who pick crops or sew our clothes. Balance, is looking at a Mark Rothko painting in the National Gallery — it all floats. Unlike the consequences of war, the size of the canvas is perfectly clear. I cry in my sleep and dream of dolphins caught in a fisherman's net. They are serenaded in death by a sea who willingly gives them up, an offering of peace. Why don't we have the wisdom of the lava flows that know exactly where to stop, elegantly, before a few green blades of grass?

Breathing Forward in America

James is the Americanized name
of my D.C. cabbie, who fled soil-starved
Nigeria, to drive me to the Hyatt from the airport.
The militias that killed his wife and children missed
him as he had gone to Lagos for work.

The angels say we imprint our path
before we arrive as babies. I chose stones
slung across my back in guilt.

Candelaria, who cleans my toilet at the hotel,
came from El Salvador. She is a doctor.
Better a half-life with little dignity in work
than the scripts of violence tattooed on her flesh.

Their nightmares live in screams
I don't hear. Survival
memories are headstones
dedicated to savagery.

Music is what remains of their attempts
to breathe forward in America. James' long
fingers tap the steering wheel to a tune
in a language I have never heard.

Candelaria sways with a Mijares ballad
as she vacuums. I want
to believe my hand is free
of any nails I might have hammered
into their flesh,
but I know this cannot be true.

43

BLOOMS

Talking to my daughter
smells like the times when everyone else's story
is more important than yours
and you are the star of the event
or the reason for the funeral notice.

I tell her life is like inhaling large breaths
of wildflowers that bloom
in the desert after the monsoons.

Unpredictable and often misunderstood
she pretends not to listen,
doesn't look up from her Hollywood magazine.

I play her a recording of B.B. King.
I kneel down in front of her.
When you hear a howl in the Blues,
close your eyes
imagine a forensic pathologist
gazing at a human ribcage
wondering where the heart ended up.

She sighs the irony that can't be held in her hands.

ASKING THE DESERT IF IT IS TIME TO COME HOME

Hiking in Gates Pass, Sahuaro National Forest

Ants in the desert mean patience.
They trek slowly over my shoes.

A mountain curves with the soft
movement of a woman's
breast, fondling cloud mist
to her peaks. The sahuaros climb
to the top in various shades, long of shadow.
Eagle crests the horizon,
dives in my direction
calls to me and says, ride –

Standing on a mother rock
in the middle of a wash recently cleansed
by a flash flood, I watch Cardinal land on the ocotillo
in bloom beside me. Its silhouette
laces my leg. A coyote runs out
of nowhere in front of me,
wise ones whisper through wind,
coyote brings messages.

Out loud I ask, are you trickster
or creator of new universes
in this Tohono O'odham land?
I see the prickly pear has ripe
purple fruit ready to pick.
The jumping cholla slings
its wad of thorns into my legs.

Which is it, Coyote—
thorns or a return to fruit?

Unsheltered

The village men of San Pedro
finish placing flat rocks
on the road to make it passable
as the storm arrives.
Arterial mud connects life
from the end of one village
to the next. The rain's stone music
mixes with the contralto
mud to fall on the salmon
swimming in the narrow creek
by the road. Despite the falling
sound, there is too little water
for it to reach the curve
by the pink rock where it was born.

Death before renewal.
Homeless totems,
these rocks by the road,
some so small,
they reposition in the wind.
Some so large,
they bear the look of nuns
who have denied their bodies love,
unmovable gray sentries
who favor pain.
There is so much an unsheltered
Jabiru stork can see in the rain.

WILLOW CONVERSATIONS

The lowest branch of the willow tree,
exposed,
different than its siblings,
separated by an obvious space
the way love and death can take up
opposite sides of the body.

Two types of wind conversation compete.
The lower unadorned, converse in whispers
with like-minded leaves.
The upper clusters mix madly,
dance tangos and laugh unashamed.

Silence swallows all words.

IV

THE HEART TELLS LIES

Writer's Block

Words form hoof marks
that settle on skin,
then shrink, or get screamed
into the frontal lobes.

During the foreplay of thoughts
to page, muscle tissues flex my hand,
cleave to my jaw hard,
or fester in tributaries
like champagne bubbles
toasted to the lonely.

My body knows the heart tells lies.
Only what gets written
understands what I really love—
a palaver not enslaved
to the linear guard dogs
of time and money.

Yanked hair draped on a sumptuous cactus
is a hysterical act of word denial on my part.
Language must seep through
skin sentinels to ink.

Caged mischief must be set free
or the coroner will discover in my innards,
the acuity of a spider threading its fly.

BODY WINTER

Full of thorns, the paloverde branch
remains frozen inside my crescent ribs.
A white-ribbon carving of my face,
peeled and framed in black clouds
is how I carry your memory.
The continuous wash of the blue dishes
helps erase the small lines on fingers
that once gently traced your eyebrows.

With a green broom and silver dust pan,
I gather crucifixes from the time
I opened love with an axe,
hacked my way past
unthinking spires of loneliness,
a lynching now safely sewn
with coarse stitches from my belly
to my left clavicle bone.

The past taunts for death by the sword,
but my love letters
remain green with innocence.

DEATH ANNIVERSARY

For Yaya

Today, the blue walls of my garden
sharpen the sadness rapier against my chest wall.
The frost-crispened ficus slurs
its greeting after the morning rain,
cream layered leaves monotonous,
daring new green to come from within.

The sparrows and mourning doves
line the telephone wire in a bizarre
Morse code of one-note loneliness.
I sense your ether hands
on my shoulders and head,
an attempt to remove ash shade.

It is a moment of opulence, this recollection.
A time to trace the half moon
on my fingernails,
and as every year, match
my heartbeat to Thais' Meditation.

Today, I will eat your favorite Paella,
and when my fork forgets
to stop at the black olive pit,
the perfect encapsulation
of funeral rules,
I will pierce its skin twice
with remembrance.

The burnt bougainvillea,
is the only swatch of color
left in the chiaroscuro.

THE ALCHEMY OF LUST

A single bougainvillea branch hangs
away from the garden wall, its shape
suggests a man. Fuchsia and thorns
wanting to enter the window, but cannot.

My neighbor's black tom cat
readies to pounce on unsuspecting sparrow,
as if my garden were a bar
and all the birds lined up for a beer,
a Joe, ready to pick off the blondes.

I remember a kiss behind my left ear,
yellow rununculus in bloom
the solo branch as lonely as love.

Night Mothers

The moon paints
chaparral thorns
on my breasts.

I hold them up to the night
for the many who suckled
and gave nothing back.

My hands encircle
to embrace my night mothers,
pale jacaranda aureolas.

Reflective moons,
the twin sisters hang exhausted
from feeding so many.

Age has weighed them down,
nipples show the bites
of children and frank betrayals.

I brush the silver-painted hairs
away from my eyes.
What of my own sustenance?

Sometimes late at night when
the jasmine and copal are sweetest
the breast sisters wander

from this land of the dead,
bright and erect once more,
beacons to *Esperanza*.

54

MOTHER WAIL

The mother-beast is scorched,
I will not follow my daughter into hell.
Systematically, I remove the guitar
strings, destroy the case
that once held her wood,
her life form, in the cradles
of my elbows.

The corpse of her shadow
is a mourning coat I must wear.
It allows the ghosts of all mothers
to walk right through me.
Its dark black leather
smell magnifies the fear
tattooed on the softest skin
beneath my left breast.

La Llorona asks why I don't
continue to search for her?
I preserve her memory in blue
enameled butterflies
and the possibility
of cherry blossoms in winter.
She wails welts on my ribs,
until my insides look
like a pock scarred moon.

September Monsoon

If a glass shatters in Madrid,
does anyone hear in the desert?
My brother and sister ghosts
know the answer to this koan as they listen
with me to poems of adversity on the radio.
The monsoon winds sway tall ocotillo
fingers, green slender air rockets,
religious answers that point
skyward in different directions.
Do I follow more the sun or moon moments today?
The sun's male energy provides
steady sustenance, but the moon's deeper ties
to water are potential rain clouds
that pause overhead in shadows of promise.
My nipples become erect,
as if trying to hold on to a man's touch,
a reaction to the sudden wind.
They are as fragile as baby finches
landing on orange and yellow Mexican
Birds of Paradise blossoms,
tenuous holds, like the kisses I once
couldn't be bothered to count.
The flutter of ruby hummingbirds
seek encouragement from the desert,
rapid hearts for my thoughts.
Secrets in gray and purple sunrise
bow in waves of paloverde branches
to challenge the wind.
I see the very long shadow I cast
when my hands raise themselves,
sometimes in prayer, sometimes in judgment.

Suddenly Blind, A Time to Receive

For Diane Frank

You have discovered
the eyes are only one way of letting go
of life, an unforgiving landscape
partitioned in barbed wire.

There is no longer a need
to darken the lamps,
the world is now precise in its boxes.
You are the comet's tail
shining most brightly
in what you have left behind.

Eyes inward can dust
off the catwalks of memory,
hands can rediscover simple things:
a signature, the eyes of a child,
the sacredness of leaves
still attached to an orange.

A time for innuendos in conversation,
to hear the music of the conch.
A time to listen for the heartbeats
still in the fog of the seeing.

OTHER ROADS BEG TRAVEL

I called out to you to stop your journey
in a seemingly opposite direction
from mine for just an evening of rowing
on the lake. Why or why not
is irrelevant. All my journeys
lead back to Spain and away from Rome.

In 1795, the Spanish granted navigation rights
to merchants on the Mississippi.
Who now remembers this detail?
The flow still goes to the delta
where devastation and harvest occur
season after season. Nothing is new.

So why is your face beside my cheek
cupped upwards like an angel,
so prohibitive? My head is the bottom
of a boat that just wants to glide smoothly
in the water after a summer rain.
The straps that hold our
oars in place prevent the world
from slipping your hand to mine.
Your essence, my essence remain
afloat, above the side board,
whispers pass through pores,
touching everything but my voice.

I write them down in my head's suitcase
so they outlast the sorrows
exchanged side by side
facing the wet half-moon.

PRIVATE DÍA DE LOS MUERTOS

I scatter rose petals of the previous year
among the pictures of my dead,
know that I must talk about my missing daughter,
the lynching of hatred at my work
and how after all these years,
I still don't fit credibly among the living.

I create my altar, word arrows
finally release from the taut
strung bow of my throat,
and emerge with the lighting
of the candles to the *Virgen de Guadalupe*.
The noiseless vocabulary stockpiled
inside my latch cracks open,
anguish no longer stockwire held to my bones.

In front of the marigolds
and yellow chrysanthemums, confessions emerge
about the lack of love on my skin.
I speak for hours about my days,
the hope-laden laughter at baptisms,
the bougainvillea blooms in my garden,
red finches and baby mourning doves.

The copal incense curls around my voice,
dances with my breath and integrates
the torn pieces of moonlight back into myself.
A scent of pine, a wind caress, is my dead
brother, his smell when he visits my dreams.

Before they leave,
fully refreshed on holy water, bread
and rosaries, I ask my *muertos* to teach me
the success psalms for living on dirt,
ask the stars for sensuous potential,
animate this oyster shell called skin
to dance a tango before it closes its pores,
heal the hole in the middle of my sunflower heart.

COUNTING WINTERS

I believe it more appropriate
to count our ages in winters
because to survive the cold
is no small thing.

The yearly hoarfrost
makes my skin look more and more
like tea-spotted wrinkled silk.
I want the same things now

I did at twenty:
to wake up with the curve
of a loving hand on my breast
before all that is left
are slapping sounds
dead palm fronds,
as desert wind shudders.

My Intuition

La intuición enwraps my body
like a second self, constantly changing form.
Territorial to my skin,
her history is shackled to fist and ankle.

She senses the diminishing
vital signs of my brother
who dies hundreds of miles
from my perch on the airplane.

More than once,
she repelled violence.
Once, I dated a dangerous Greek, *la sabia*
tracked me like a she-wolf sniffing her cave.

When I pretend she is an easy
slip I can put on or off,
I hear her laughing at me,
cicadas in a Texas spring.

La intuición hears the dead
talk to my marrow.
At night she lends my ghosts
lips and invisible arms.

Everyone must know her,
she is the unspoken echo
of my voice, in conversation
with the shadow of its words.

UNKNOWN PATTERN

"If I am to enter the unknown pattern each moment gives, at least I can enter also, the comfort of water."
                    —Margaret Gibson

I shout stone,
and other solid
words that sustain
hope above the noise —
spontaneous life, that jazz
of quick, small and long breaths
that get us by cuts.

My spirit bleeds in tendrils of ash
that peel unnoticed
from the tree, one slash
a requiem for sorrow,
like a knife cutting in one
swoop the plump outline
of an orange.

Sorrow descends to the ground
in wasted color,
buried under the cold
until the rake arrives
to arrange neat piles.

I seek a swallow's refuge in a storm,
where rocks capture seawater
in pumice holes,
and sounds are as predictable
as wave's froth,
memory, a sonata.

TORO FROM EUSKADI

Paseíllo

I am the bull born of Basques
bred to die this day
in three stages, youth
and old age compressed
into moments inside a bull ring.

The first to parade, I stir
the dust with my hooves
salute the crowd, bow my head
and toss blessings
with my horns.
On my back, a coronet
of yellow roses, the colors
of my house to honor
my first paseo. A gladiator
in awe of glory, alone
for now, warm with applause,
sunshine, and already
thirsty for water.

Tercio de Varas

The first ferocity taunt
comes from a blindfolded horse
in padding with a man-beast
taller than myself who lances
my hump, the strength
of my back. An old woman
tosses a white rose on the ground

between us, as if its white
petals mixed with dirt are the saints
deciding who lives this day.

Tercio de Banderillas

I search the crowd for the *presidente*
of this fight. His face anxious
for the symphony, still deciding
if my right ear will be awarded
to the torero. The breeze
cools first blood on my skin,
this no longer
a practice with *novilleros*.

He advances with sticks
festooned in gold and blue,
the colors of St. Joan.
I believe the harpooned hooks
are aimed at my heart.

With one *banderilla* in each
hand, curved upward,
in the stance of a conductor
greeting his orchestra, the man's
sudden downward movement
claws my haunch,
the blood quick
as the castanets of Spain.

I am supposed to fight
the pain in my back, pierce
with my horn a suit of lights,
a thousand sequins and beads

that illuminate a man, too thin
to escape me completely.

Tercio de muerte, la faena.

And now we finally dance
the *Pasodoble,* so close together
my blood stains his suit.
He learns my horns,
I study his feet.
I smell his sweat,
he breathes my scent.
I move with the gasps of the crowd,
Olé.

The blood from the *banderillas*
stings my eyes, a toss
of my head clears my vision.
My right hoof lifts to paw
the ground, the anticipation silence
comforts my ear. I charge
to the left, away from the cape
send dust to the *matador's* face,
Olé.

The dance faena is slowing.
The noise of the crowd now
only the buzz of a bumblebee.
My soul is ready to mix
with the sunset. I ask forgiveness
for weakness and seek
permission from Euzkadi
to die with haste.

From behind the red cape
comes the sword, the *estocada*.
Torero faces me, his sword arm
high, his white suit now stained
in places, his blood or mine?
Repentance crushed in a precise
stab so hidden, I see the rise of his feet.

This is the *corrida,*
a run, a circle dance,
a song of brave death.
The crowd's red and yellow roses
begin to descend,
the petals beg my death.

The last *Olé* is sung,
I fall, the pageant complete.
Madre llevame a casa.

PUBLICATION ACKNOWLEDGMENTS

Grateful acknowledgment is made to the following publications in which some of the poems in this collection previously appeared, at times in earlier versions:

Crab Orchard Review, Vol. 12 No. 2: "San Fernando Cathedral, San Antonio de Bejar, Día de los Muertos."

Eden River Press: Anthology on Home: "Breathing Forward in America"

Pudding House Press: Chapbook, **This Stone Will Speak** that contains the following poems: "This Stone Will Speak," "From Heaven to Life," "My Moon," "Women are Doors," "Via Sacra," "Dreaming History," "Quizás," "Afternoon at the Ranch in Oregon With my Anglo Relatives," "My Mother Wants me to Explain," "San Fernando Cathedral, San Antonio, de Bejar, Día de los Muertos," "St. Francis in Mesilla," "Toro from Euzkadi," "Alfonsina Walks into the Sea," "September Monsoon," "Private Día de los Muertos," "Other Roads Beg Travel," "Asking the Desert if it is time to Come Home," and "Socks."

Sante Lucia Books: After Shocks, Anthology on the Poetry of Recovery: "Breathing Forward in America"

Red Hen Press: Letters to the World, An Anthology of the Wompo List Serve: "Snail"

Best Poem.Org Edited by Adam Penna: "Mother Wail"

Sin Fronteras Literatry Magazine Vol 13: "Corset"

Poetry Society of Connecticut, Brodine–Brodinsky third place winner, "A Woman's Hands in a Time of War."

About the Poet

L isha Adela García is a bilingual, bicultural poet who has México, the United States and that land in between (Spanglish) in her work. She has an MFA from Vermont College in Creative Writing and currently resides in Arizona with her beloved four-legged children. Lisha is a simultaneous interpreter and translator and is influenced by the American Southwest, the ghosts that haunt her labyrinth and border culture. She has translated, *Will of Light* by reknowned Mexican poet, Luis Armenta Malpica. *This Stone Will Speak*, a chapbook, has been published and is available at Pudding House Press. This book was a finalist for the Andrés Montoya Prize at the University of Notre Dame. Lisha, also has a Masters degree for the left side of her brain in International Management, from the Thunderbird School of Global Management.

Printed in the United States of America

www.ingramcontent.com/pod-product-compliance
Lightning Source LLC
Chambersburg PA
CBHW032028090426
42741CB00006B/769